SELECTED POEMS

Robinson Jeffers

*Selected
Poems*

VINTAGE BOOKS

A Division of Random House

New York

✳ Contents

SELECTED POEMS

✳ To the Stone-Cutters

Stone-cutters fighting time with marble, you foredefeated
Challengers of oblivion
Eat cynical earnings, knowing rock splits, records fall
    down,
The square-limbed Roman letters
Scale in the thaws, wear in the rain. The poet as well
Builds his monument mockingly;
For man will be blotted out, the blithe earth die, the
    brave sun
Die blind and blacken to the heart:
Yet stones have stood for a thousand years, and pained
    thoughts found
The honey of peace in old poems.

✳ Continent's End

At the equinox when the earth was veiled in a late rain,
  wreathed with wet poppies, waiting spring,
The ocean swelled for a far storm and beat its boundary,
  the ground-swell shook the beds of granite:

I gazing at the boundaries of granite and spray, the es-
  tablished sea-marks, felt behind me
Mountain and plain, the immense breadth of the conti-
  nent, before me the mass and doubled stretch of
  water.

I said: You yoke the Aleutian seal-rocks with the lava
  and coral sowings that flower the south,
Over your flood the life that sought the sunrise faces ours
  that has followed the evening star.

The long migrations meet across you and it is nothing
  to you, you have forgotten us, mother.
You were much younger when we crawled out of the
  womb and lay in the sun's eye on the tideline.

It was long and long ago; we have grown proud since
  then and you have grown bitter; life retains
Your mobile soft unquiet strength; and envies hardness,
  the insolent quietness of stone.

The tides are in our veins, we still mirror the stars, life
  is your child, but there is in me
Older and harder than life and more impartial, the eye
  that watched before there was an ocean.

That watched you fill your beds out of the condensation
   of thin vapor and watched you change them,
That saw you soft and violent wear your boundaries
   down, eat rock, shift places with the continents.

Mother, though my song's measure is like your surf-
   beat's ancient rhythm I never learned it of you.
Before there was any water there were tides of fire, both
   our tones flow from the older fountain.

✳ Night

The ebb slips from the rock, the sunken
Tide-rocks lift streaming shoulders
Out of the slack, the slow west
Sombering its torch; a ship's light
Shows faintly, far out,
Over the weight of the prone ocean
On the low cloud.

Over the dark mountain, over the dark pinewood,
Down the long dark valley along the shrunken river,
Returns the splendor without rays, the shining of shadow,
Peace-bringer, the matrix of all shining and quieter of
    shining.
Where the shore widens on the bay she opens dark wings
And the ocean accepts her glory. O soul worshipful of
    her
You like the ocean have grave depths where she dwells
    always,
And the film of waves above that takes the sun takes also
Her, with more love. The sun-lovers have a blond fa-
    vorite,
A father of lights and noises, wars, weeping and laughter,
Hot labor, lust and delight and the other blemishes.
    Quietness
Flows from her deeper fountain; and he will die; and she
    is immortal.

Far off from here the slender
Flocks of the mountain forest
Move among stems like towers
Of the old redwoods to the stream,
No twig crackling; dip shy

Wild muzzles into the mountain water
Among the dark ferns.

O passionately at peace you being secure will pardon
The blasphemies of glowworms, the lamp in my tower,
    the fretfulness
Of cities, the cressets of the planets, the pride of the
    stars.
This August night in a rift of cloud Antares reddens,
The great one, the ancient torch, a lord among lost chil-
    dren,
The earth's orbit doubled would not girdle his greatness,
    one fire
Globed, out of grasp of the mind enormous; but to you
    O Night
What? Not a spark? What flicker of a spark in the faint
    far glimmer
Of a lost fire dying in the desert, dim coals of a sand-pit
    the Bedouins
Wandered from at dawn . . . Ah singing prayer to
    what gulfs tempted
Suddenly are you more lost? To us the near-hand moun-
    tain
Be a measure of height, the tide-worn cliff at the sea-gate
    a measure of continuance.

The tide, moving the night's
Vastness with lonely voices,
Turns, the deep dark-shining
Pacific leans on the land,
Feeling his cold strength
To the outmost margins: you Night will resume
The stars in your time.

O passionately at peace when will that tide draw shore-
ward?
Truly the spouting fountains of light, Antares, Arcturus,
Tire of their flow, they sing one song but they think
silence.
The striding winter giant Orion shines, and dreams dark-
ness.
And life, the flicker of men and moths and the wolf on
the hill,
Though furious for continuance, passionately feeding,
passionately
Remaking itself upon its mates, remembers deep inward
The calm mother, the quietness of the womb and the egg,
The primal and the latter silences: dear Night it is
memory
Prophesies, prophecy that remembers, the charm of the
dark.
And I and my people, we are willing to love the four-
score years
Heartily; but as a sailor loves the sea, when the helm is
for harbor.

Have men's minds changed,
Or the rock hidden in the deep of the waters of the soul
Broken the surface? A few centuries
Gone by, was none dared not to people
The darkness beyond the stars with harps and habita-
tions.
But now, dear is the truth. Life is grown sweeter and
lonelier,
And death is no evil.

✳ Shine, Perishing Republic

While this America settles in the mould of its vulgarity,
    heavily thickening to empire,
And protest, only a bubble in the molten mass, pops
    and sighs out, and the mass hardens,

I sadly smiling remember that the flower fades to make
    fruit, the fruit rots to make earth.
Out of the mother; and through the spring exultances,
    ripeness and decadence; and home to the mother.

You making haste haste on decay: not blameworthy; life
    is good, be it stubbornly long or suddenly
A mortal splendor: meteors are not needed less than
    mountains: shine, perishing republic.

But for my children, I would have them keep their dis-
    tance from the thickening center; corruption
Never has been compulsory, when the cities lie at the
    monster's feet there are left the mountains.

And boys, be in nothing so moderate as in love of man,
    a clever servant, insufferable master.
There is the trap that catches noblest spirits, that caught
    —they say—God, when he walked on earth.

✳ Apology for Bad Dreams

I

In the purple light, heavy with redwood, the slopes drop
        seaward,
Headlong convexities of forest, drawn in together to the
        step ravine. Below, on the sea-cliff,
A lonely clearing; a little field of corn by the streamside;
        a roof under spared trees. Then the ocean
Like a great stone someone has cut to a sharp edge and
        polished to shining. Beyond it, the fountain
And furnace of incredible light flowing up from the sunk
        sun. In the little clearing a woman
Is punishing a horse; she had tied the halter to a sapling
        at the edge of the wood, but when the great whip
Clung to the flanks the creature kicked so hard she
        feared he would snap the halter; she called from
        the house
The young man her son; who fetched a chain tie-rope,
        they working together
Noosed the small rusty links round the horse's tongue
And tied him by the swollen tongue to the tree.
Seen from this height they are shrunk to insect size.
Out of all human relation. You cannot distinguish
The blood dripping from where the chain is fastened,
The beast shuddering; but the thrust neck and the legs
Far apart. You can see the whip fall on the flanks . . .
The gesture of the arm. You cannot see the face of the
        woman.
The enormous light beats up out of the west across the
        cloudbars of the trade-wind. The ocean
Darkens, the high clouds brighten, the hills darken to-
        gether. Unbridled and unbelievable beauty

Covers the evening world . . . not covers, grows appar-
ent out of it, as Venus down there grows out
From the lit sky. What said the prophet? "I create good:
and I create evil: I am the Lord."

II

This coast crying out for tragedy like all beautiful places,
(The quiet ones ask for quieter suffering: but here the
granite cliff the gaunt cypresses crown
Demands what victim? The dykes of red lava and black
what Titan? The hills like pointed flames
Beyond Soberanes, the terrible peaks of the bare hills
under the sun, what immolation?)
This coast crying out for tragedy like all beautiful places:
and like the passionate spirit of humanity
Pain for its bread: God's, many victims', the painful
deaths, the horrible transfigurations: I said in my
heart,
"Better invent than suffer: imagine victims
Lest your own flesh be chosen the agonist, or you
Martyr some creature to the beauty of the place." And
I said,
"Burn sacrifices once a year to magic
Horror away from the house, this little house here
You have built over the ocean with your own hands
Beside the standing boulders: for what are we,
The beast that walks upright, with speaking lips
And little hair, to think we should always be fed,
Sheltered, intact, and self-controlled? We sooner more
liable
Than the other animals. Pain and terror, the insanities of
desire; not accidents but essential,
And crowd up from the core:" I imagined victims for
those wolves, I made them phantoms to follow,

They have hunted the phantoms and missed the house.
   It is not good to forget over what gulfs the spirit
Of the beauty of humanity, the petal of a lost flower
   blown seaward by the night-wind, floats to its quiet-
   ness.

III

Boulders blunted like an old bear's teeth break up from
   the headland; below them
All the soil is thick with shells, the tide-rock feasts of a
   dead people.
Here the granite flanks are scarred with ancient fire, the
   ghosts of the tribe
Crouch in the nights beside the ghost of a fire, they try
   to remember the sunlight,
Light has died out of their skies. These have paid some-
   thing for the future
Luck of the country, while we living keep old griefs in
   memory: though God's
Envy is not a likely fountain of ruin, to forget evils calls
   down
Sudden reminders from the cloud: remembered deaths
   be our redeemers;
Imagined victims our salvation: white as the half moon
   at midnight
Someone flamelike passed me, saying, "I am Tamar
   Cauldwell, I have my desire,"
Then the voice of the sea returned, when she had gone
   by, the stars to their towers.
. . . Beautiful country burn again, Point Pinos down to
   the Sur Rivers
Burn as before with bitter wonders, land and ocean and
   the Carmel water.

IV

He brays humanity in a mortar to bring the savor
From the bruised root: a man having bad dreams, who
  invents victims, is only the ape of that God.
He washes it out with tears and many waters, calcines it
  with fire in the red crucible,
Deforms it, makes it horrible to itself: the spirit flies out
  and stands naked, he sees the spirit,
He takes it in the naked ecstasy; it breaks in his hand,
  the atom is broken, the power that massed it
Cries to the power that moves the stars, "I have come
  home to myself, behold me.
I bruised myself in the flint mortar and burnt me
In the red shell, I tortured myself, I flew forth,
Stood naked of myself and broke me in fragments,
And here am I moving the stars that are me."
I have seen these ways of God: I know of no reason
For fire and change and torture and the old returnings.
He being sufficient might be still. I think they admit no
  reason; they are the ways of my love.
Unmeasured power, incredible passion, enormous craft:
  no thought apparent but burns darkly
Smothered with its own smoke in the human brain-vault:
  no thought outside: a certain measure in phenom-
  ena:
The fountains of the boiling stars, the flowers on the
  foreland, the ever-returning roses of dawn.

✳ Roan Stallion

The dog barked; then the woman stood in the doorway,
     and hearing iron strike stone down the steep road
Covered her head with a black shawl and entered the
     light rain; she stood at the turn of the road.
A nobly formed woman; erect and strong as a new
     tower; the features stolid and dark
But sculptured into a strong grace; straight nose with
     a high bridge, firm and wide eyes, full chin,
Red lips; she was only a fourth part Indian; a Scottish
     sailor had planted her in young native earth,
Spanish and Indian, twenty-one years before. He had
     named her California when she was born;
That was her name; and had gone north.
                                   She heard the
     hooves and wheels come nearer, up the steep road.
The buckskin mare, leaning against the breastpiece,
     plodded into sight round the wet bank.
The pale face of the driver followed; the burnt-out eyes;
     they had fortune in them. He sat twisted
On the seat of the old buggy, leading a second horse by
     a long halter, a roan, a big one,
That stepped daintily; by the swell of the neck, a stallion.
     "What have you got, Johnny?" "Maskerel's stallion.
Mine now. I won him last night, I had very good luck."
     He was quite drunk. "They bring their mares up
     here now.
I keep this fellow. I got money besides, but I'll not show
     you." "Did you buy something, Johnny,
For our Christine? Christmas comes in two days,
     Johnny." "By God, forgot," he answered laughing.
"Don't tell Christine it's Christmas; after while I get her
     something, maybe." But California:

"I shared your luck when you lost: you lost *me* once,
    Johnny, remember? Tom Dell had me two nights
Here in the house: other times we've gone hungry: now
    that you've won, Christine will have her Christmas.
We share your luck, Johnny. You give me money, I go
    down to Monterey to-morrow,
Buy presents for Christine, come back in the evening.
    Next day Christmas." "You have wet ride," he
    answered
Giggling. "Here money. Five dollar; ten; twelve dollar.
    You buy two bottles of rye whiskey for Johnny."
"All right. I go to-morrow."
                      He was an outcast Hol-
    lander; not old, but shriveled with bad living.
The child Christine inherited from his race blue eyes,
    from his life a wizened forehead; she watched
From the house-door her father lurch out of the buggy
    and lead with due respect the stallion
To the new corral, the strong one; leaving the wearily
    breathing buckskin mare to his wife to unharness.

Storm in the night; the rain on the thin shakes of the
    roof like the ocean on rock streamed battering;
    once thunder
Walked down the narrow canyon into Carmel valley and
    wore away westward; Christine was wakeful
With fears and wonders; her father lay too deep for
    storm to touch him.
                      Dawn comes late in the year's
    dark,
Later into the crack of a canyon under redwoods; and
    California slipped from bed
An hour before it; the buckskin would be tired; there
    was a little barley, and why should Johnny

Feed all the barley to his stallion? That is what he would
    do. She tip-toed out of the room.
Leaving her clothes, he'd waken if she waited to put
    them on, and passed from the door of the house
Into the dark of the rain; the big black drops were cold
    through the thin shift, but the wet earth
Pleasant under her naked feet. There was a pleasant
    smell in the stable; and moving softly,
Touching things gently with the supple bend of the un-
    clothed body, was pleasant. She found a box,
Filled it with sweet dry barley and took it down to the
    old corral. The little mare sighed deeply
At the rail in the wet darkness; and California returning
    between two redwoods up to the house
Heard the happy jaws grinding the grain. Johnny could
    mind the pigs and chickens. Christine called to her
When she entered the house, but slept again under her
    hand. She laid the wet night-dress on a chair-back
And stole into the bedroom to get her clothes. A plank
    creaked, and he wakened. She stood motionless
Hearing him stir in the bed. When he was quiet she
    stooped after her shoes, and he said softly,
"What are you doing? Come back to bed." "It's late,
    I'm going to Monterey, I must hitch up."
"You come to bed first. I been away three days. I give
    you money, I take back the money
And what you do in town then?" She sighed sharply and
    came to the bed.
                        He reaching his hands from it
Felt the cool curve and firmness of her flank, and half
    rising caught her by the long wet hair.
She endured, and to hasten the act she feigned desire;
    she had not for long, except in dream, felt it.

Yesterday's drunkenness made him sluggish and exact-
    ing; she saw, turning her head sadly,
The windows were bright gray with dawn; he embraced
    her still, stopping to talk about the stallion.
At length she was permitted to put on her clothes. Clear
    daylight over the steep hills;
Gray-shining cloud over the tops of the redwoods; the
    winter stream sang loud; the wheels of the buggy
Slipped in deep slime, ground on washed stones at the
    road-edge. Down the hill the wrinkled river smoth-
    ered the ford.
You must keep to the bed of stones: she knew the way
    by willow and alder: the buckskin halted mid-
    stream,
Shuddering, the water her own color washing up to the
    traces; but California, drawing up
Her feet out of the whirl onto the seat of the buggy
    swung the whip over the yellow water
And drove to the road.
                  All morning the clouds were rac-
    ing northward like a river. At noon they thickened.
When California faced the southwind home from Mon-
    terey it was heavy with level rainfall.
She looked seaward from the foot of the valley; red rays
    cried sunset from a trumpet of streaming
Cloud over Lobos, the southwest occident of the solstice.
    Twilight came soon, but the tired mare
Feared the road more than the whip. Mile after mile of
    slow gray twilight.
                  Then, quite suddenly, darkness.
"Christine will be asleep. It is Christmas Eve. The ford.
    That hour of daylight wasted this morning!"
She could see nothing; she let the reins lie on the dash-

board and knew at length by the cramp of the
wheels
And the pitch down, they had reached it. Noise of wheels
on stones, plashing of hooves in water; a world
Of sounds; no sight; the gentle thunder of water; the
mare snorting, dipping her head, one knew,
To look for footing, in the blackness, under the stream.
The hushing and creaking of the sea-wind
In the passion of invisible willows.

The mare stood still;
the woman shouted to her; spared whip,
For a false leap would lose the track of the ford. She
stood. "The baby's things," thought California,
"Under the seat: the water will come over the floor";
and rising in the midst of the water
She tilted the seat; fetched up the doll, the painted
wooden chickens, the woolly bear, the book
Of many pictures, the box of sweets: she brought them
all from under the seat and stored them, trembling,
Under her clothes, about the breasts, under the arms;
the corners of the cardboard boxes
Cut into the soft flesh; but with a piece of rope for a
girdle and wound about the shoulders
All was made fast. The mare stood still as if asleep in
the midst of the water. Then California
Reached out a hand over the stream and fingered her
rump; the solid wet convexity of it
Shook like the beat of a great heart. "What are you wait-
ing for?" But the feel of the animal surface
Had wakened a dream, obscured real danger with a
dream of danger. "What for? For the water-stallion
To break out of the stream, that is what the rump strains
for, him to come up flinging foam sidewise,

Fore-hooves in air, crush me and the rig and curl over
    his woman." She flung out with the whip then,
The mare plunged forward. The buggy drifted sidelong:
    was she off ground? Swimming? No: by the
    splashes.
The driver, a mere prehensile instinct, clung to the side-
    irons of the seat and felt the force
But not the coldness of the water, curling over her knees,
    breaking up to the waist
Over her body. They'd turned. The mare had turned up
    stream and was wallowing back into shoal water.
Then California dropped her forehead to her knees,
    having seen nothing, feeling a danger,
And felt the brute weight of a branch of alder, the
    pendulous light leaves brush her bent neck
Like a child's fingers. The mare burst out of water and
    stopped on the slope to the ford. The woman
    climbed down
Between the wheels and went to her head. "Poor Dora,"
    she called her by her name, "there, Dora. Quietly,"
And led her around, there was room to turn on the mar-
    gin, the head to the gentle thunder of the water.
She crawled on hands and knees, felt for the ruts, and
    shifted the wheels into them. "You can see, Dora.
I can't. But this time you'll go through it." She climbed
    into the seat and shouted angrily. The mare
Stopped, her two forefeet in the water. She touched with
    the whip. The mare plodded ahead and halted.
Then California thought of prayer: "Dear little Jesus,
Dear baby Jesus born to-night, your head was shining
Like silver candles. I've got a baby too, only a girl. You
    had light wherever you walked.
Dear baby Jesus give me light." Light streamed: rose,

gold, rich purple, hiding the ford like a curtain.

The gentle thunder of water was a noise of wing-feathers,
    the fans of paradise lifting softly.

The child afloat on radiance had a baby face, but the
    angels had birds' heads, hawks' heads,

Bending over the baby, weaving a web of wings about
    him. He held in the small fat hand

A little snake with golden eyes, and California could see
    clearly on the under radiance

The mare's pricked ears, a sharp black fork against the
    shining light-fall. But it dropped; the light of heaven

Frightened poor Dora. She backed; swung up the water,

And nearly oversetting the buggy turned and scrambled
    backward; the iron wheel-tires rang on boulders.

Then California weeping climbed between the wheels.
    Her wet clothes and the toys packed under

Dragged her down with their weight; she stripped off
    cloak and dress and laid the baby's things in the
    buggy;

Brought Johnny's whiskey out from under the seat;
    wrapped all in the dress, bottles and toys, and tied
    them

Into a bundle that would sling over her back. She un-
    harnessed the mare, hurting her fingers

Against the swollen straps and the wet buckles. She tied
    the pack over her shoulders, the cords

Crossing her breasts, and mounted. She drew up her
    shift about her waist and knotted it, naked thighs

Clutching the sides of the mare, bare flesh to the wet
    withers, and caught the mane with her right hand,

The looped-up bridle-reins in the other. "Dora, the baby
    gives you light." The blinding radiance

Hovered the ford. "Sweet baby Jesus give us light."
    Cataracts of light and Latin singing
Fell through the willows; the mare snorted and reared:
    the roar and thunder of the invisible water;
The night shaking open like a flag, shot with the flashes;
    the baby face hovering; the water
Beating over her shoes and stockings up to the bare
    thighs; and over them, like a beast
Lapping her belly; the wriggle and pitch of the mare
    swimming; the drift, the sucking water; the blinding
Light above and behind with not a gleam before, in the
    throat of darkness; the shock of the fore-hooves
Striking bottom, the struggle and surging lift of the
    haunches. She felt the water streaming off her
From the shoulders down; heard the great strain and sob
    of the mare's breathing, heard the horseshoes grind
    on gravel.
When California came home the dog at the door snuffed
    at her without barking; Christine and Johnny
Both were asleep; she did not sleep for hours, but kin-
    dled fire and knelt patiently over it,
Shaping and drying the dear-bought gifts for Christmas
    morning.

She hated (she thought) the proud-necked stallion.
He'd lean the big twin masses of his breast on the rail,
    his red-brown eyes flash the white crescents,
She admired him then, she hated him for his uselessness,
    serving nothing
But Johnny's vanity. Horses were too cheap to breed.
    She thought, if he could range in freedom,
Shaking the red-roan mane for a flag on the bare hills.

                            A man
    brought up a mare in April;

Then California, though she wanted to watch, stayed
   with Christine indoors. When the child fretted
The mother told her once more about the miracle of the
   ford; her prayer to the little Jesus
The Christmas Eve when she was bringing the gifts
   home; the appearance, the lights, the Latin singing,
The thunder of wing-feathers and water, the shining
   child, the cataracts of splendor down the darkness.
"A little baby," Christine asked, "the God is a baby?"
   "The child of God. That was his birthday.
His mother was named Mary: we pray to her too: God
   came to her. He was not the child of a man
Like you or me. God was his father: she was the stal-
   lion's wife—what did I say—God's wife,"
She said with a cry, lifting Christine aside, pacing the
   planks of the floor. "She is called more blessed
Than any woman. She was so good, she was more
   loved." "Did God live near her house?" "He lives
Up high, over the stars; he ranges on the bare blue hill
   of the sky." In her mind a picture
Flashed, of the red-roan mane shaken out for a flag on
   the bare hills, and she said quickly, "He's more
Like a great man holding the sun in his hand." Her mind
   giving her words the lie, "But no one
Knows, only the shining and the power. The power, the
   terror, the burning fire covered her over . . ."
"Was she burnt up, mother?" "She was so good and
   lovely, she was the mother of the little Jesus.
If you are good nothing will hurt you." "What did she
   think?" "She loved, she was not afraid of the
   hooves—
Hands that had made the hills and sun and moon,
   and the sea and the great redwoods, the terrible
   strength,

She gave herself without thinking." "You only saw the
    baby, mother?" "Yes, and the angels about him,
The great wild shining over the black river." Three
    times she had walked to the door, three times re-
    turned,
And now the hand that had thrice hung on the knob,
    full of prevented action, twisted the cloth
Of the child's dress that she had been mending. "Oh, oh,
    I've torn it." She struck at the child and then em-
    braced her
Fiercely, the small blonde sickly body.

                          Johnny came in,
    his face reddened as if he had stood
Near fire, his eyes triumphing. "Finished," he said, and
    looked with malice at Christine. "I go
Down valley with Jim Carrier; owes me five dollar, fif-
    teen I charge him, he brought ten in his pocket.
Has grapes on the ranch, maybe I take a barrel red wine
    instead of money. Be back to-morrow.
To-morrow night I tell you— Eh, Jim," he laughed over
    his shoulder, "I say to-morrow evening
I show her how the red fellow act, the big fellow. When
    I come home." She answered nothing, but stood
In front of the door, holding the little hand of her daugh-
    ter, in the path of sun between the redwoods,
While Johnny tied the buckskin mare behind Carrier's
    buggy, and bringing saddle and bridle tossed them
Under the seat. Jim Carrier's mare, the bay, stood with
    drooped head and started slowly, the men
Laughing and shouting at her; their voices could be
    heard down the steep road, after the noise
Of the iron-hooped wheels died from the stone. Then
    one might hear the hush of the wind in the tall
    redwoods,

The tinkle of the April brook, deep in its hollow.
                                        Humanity
        is the start of the race; I say
Humanity is the mould to break away from, the crust to
        break through, the coal to break into fire,
The atom to be split.
                        Tragedy that breaks man's face
        and a white fire flies out of it; vision that fools him
Out of his limits, desire that fools him out of his limits,
        unnatural crime, inhuman science,
Slit eyes in the mask; wild loves that leap over the walls
        of nature, the wild fence-vaulter science,
Useless intelligence of far stars, dim knowledge of the
        spinning demons that make an atom,
These break, these pierce, these deify, praising their God
        shrilly with fierce voices: not in a man's shape
He approves the praise, he that walks lightning-naked on
        the Pacific, that laces the suns with planets,
The heart of the atom with electrons: what is humanity
        in this cosmos? For him, the last
Least taint of a trace in the dregs of the solution; for
        itself, the mould to break away from, the coal
To break into fire, the atom to be split.

                                        After the child
        slept, after the leopard-footed evening
Had glided oceanward, California turned the lamp to its
        least flame and glided from the house.
She moved sighing, like a loose fire, backward and for-
        ward on the smooth ground by the door.
She heard the night-wind that draws down the valley like
        the draught in a flue under clear weather
Whisper and toss in the tall redwoods; she heard the
        tinkle of the April brook deep in its hollow.

Cooled by the night the odors that the horses had left
  behind were in her nostrils; the night
Whitened up the bare hill; a drift of coyotes by the river
  cried bitterly against moonrise;
Then California ran to the old corral, the empty one
  where they kept the buckskin mare,
And leaned, and bruised her breasts on the rail, feeling
  the sky whiten. When the moon stood over the hill
She stole to the house. The child breathed quietly. Her-
  self: to sleep? She had seen Christ in the night at
  Christmas.
The hills were shining open to the enormous night of the
  April moon: empty and empty,
The vast round backs of the bare hills? If one should
  ride up high might not the Father himself
Be seen brooding His night, cross-legged, chin in hand,
  squatting on the last dome? More likely
Leaping the hills, shaking the red-roan mane for a flag
  on the bare hills. She blew out the lamp.
Every fiber of flesh trembled with faintness when she
  came to the door; strength lacked, to wander
Afoot into the shining of the hill, high enough, high
  enough . . . the hateful face of a man had taken
The strength that might have served her, the corral was
  empty. The dog followed her, she caught him by the
  collar,
Dragged him in fierce silence back to the door of the
  house, latched him inside.
                              It was like daylight
Outdoors and she hastened without faltering down the
  footpath, through the dark fringe of twisted oak-
  brush,
To the open place in a bay of the hill. The dark strength

of the stallion had heard her coming; she heard him
Blow the shining air out of his nostrils, she saw him in
the white lake of moonlight
Move like a lion along the timbers of the fence, shaking
the nightfall
Of the great mane; his fragrance came to her; she leaned
on the fence;
He drew away from it, the hooves making soft thunder
in the trodden soil.
Wild love had trodden it, his wrestling with the stranger,
the shame of the day
Had stamped it into mire and powder when the heavy
fetlocks
Strained the soft flanks. "Oh, if I could bear you!
If I had the strength. O great God that came down to
Mary, gently you came. But I will ride him
Up into the hill, if he throws me, if he tramples me, is it
not my desire
To endure death?" She climbed the fence, pressing her
body against the rail, shaking like fever,
And dropped inside to the soft ground. He neither
threatened her with his teeth nor fled from her
coming,
And lifting her hand gently to the upflung head she
caught the strap of the headstall,
That hung under the quivering chin. She unlooped the
halter from the high strength of the neck
And the arch the storm-cloud mane hung with live dark-
ness. He stood; she crushed her breasts
On the hard shoulder, an arm over the withers, the other
under the mass of his throat, and murmuring
Like a mountain dove, "If I could bear you." No way,
no help, a gulf in nature. She murmured, "Come,

We will run on the hill. O beautiful, O beautiful," and
    led him
To the gate and flung the bars on the ground. He threw
    his head downward
To snuff at the bars; and while he stood, she catching
    mane and withers with all sudden contracture
And strength of her lithe body, leaped, clung hard, and
    was mounted. He had been ridden before; he did
    not
Fight the weight but ran like a stone falling;
Broke down the slope into the moon-glass of the stream,
    and flattened to his neck
She felt the branches of a buckeye tree fly over her, saw
    the wall of the oak-scrub
End her world: but he turned there, the matted branches
Scraped her right knee, the great slant shoulders
Laboring the hill-slope, up, up, the clear hill. Desire had
    died in her
At the first rush, the falling like death, but now it re-
    vived,
She feeling between her thighs the labor of the great
    engine, the running muscles, the hard swiftness,
She riding the savage and exultant strength of the world.
    Having topped the thicket he turned eastward,
Running less wildly; and now at length he felt the halter
    when she drew on it; she guided him upward;
He stopped and grazed on the great arch and pride of
    the hill, the silent calvary. A dwarfish oakwood
Climbed the other slope out of the dark of the unknown
    canyon beyond; the last wind-beaten bush of it
Crawled up to the height, and California slipping from
    her mount tethered him to it. She stood then,
Shaking. Enormous films of moonlight

Trailed down from the height. Space, anxious whiteness,
vastness. Distant beyond conception the shining
ocean
Lay light like a haze along the ledge and doubtful
world's end. Little vapors gleaming, and little
Darknesses on the far chart underfoot symbolized wood
and valley; but the air was the element, the moon—
Saturate arcs and spires of the air.
                              Here is solitude, here
on the calvary, nothing conscious
But the possible God and the cropped grass, no witness,
no eye but that misformed one, the moon's past
fullness.
Two figures on the shining hill, woman and stallion, she
kneeling to him, brokenly adoring.
He cropping the grass, shifting his hooves, or lifting the
long head to gaze over the world,
Tranquil and powerful. She prayed aloud, "O God, I am
not good enough, O fear, O strength, I am drag-
gled.
Johnny and other men have had me, and O clean power!
Here am I," she said, falling before him,
And crawled to his hooves. She lay a long while, as if
asleep, in reach of the fore-hooves, weeping. He
avoided
Her head and the prone body. He backed at first; but
later plucked the grass that grew by her shoulder.
The small dark head under his nostrils: a small round
stone, that smelt human, black hair growing from
it:
The skull shut the light in: it was not possible for any
eyes
To know what throbbed and shone under the sutures of
the skull, or a shell full of lightning

Had scared the roan strength, and he'd have broken
    tether, screaming, and run for the valley.
                       The atom
    bounds-breaking,
Nucleus to sun, electrons to planets, with recognition
Not praying, self-equaling, the whole to the whole, the
    microcosm
Not entering nor accepting entrance, more equally, more
    utterly, more incredibly conjugate
With the other extreme and greatness; passionately per-
    ceptive of identity. . . .
                     The fire threw up figures
And symbols meanwhile, racial myths formed and dis-
    solved in it, the phantom rulers of humanity
That without being are yet more real than what they
    are born of, and without shape, shape that which
    makes them:
The nerves and the flesh go by shadowlike, the limbs and
    the lives shadowlike, these shadows remain, these
    shadows
To whom temples, to whom churches, to whom labors
    and wars, visions and dreams are dedicate:
Out of the fire in the small round stone that black moss
    covered, a crucified man writhed up in anguish;
A woman covered by a huge beast in whose mane the
    stars were netted, sun and moon were his eyeballs,
Smiled under the unendurable violation, her throat swol-
    len with the storm and blood-flecks gleaming
On the stretched lips; a woman—no, a dark water, split
    by jets of lightning, and after a season
What floated up out of the furrowed water, a boat, a
    fish, a fire-globe?
                It had wings, the creature,

And flew against the fountain of lightning, fell burnt out
    of the cloud back to the bottomless water . . .
Figures and symbols, castlings of the fire, played in her
    brain; but the white fire was the essence,
The burning in the small round shell of bone that black
    hair covered, that lay by the hooves on the hilltop.

She rose at length, she unknotted the halter; she walked
    and led the stallion; two figures, woman and stal-
    lion,
Came down the silent emptiness of the dome of the hill,
    under the cataract of the moonlight.

The next night there was moon through cloud. Johnny
    had returned half drunk toward evening, and Cali-
    fornia
Who had known him for years with neither love nor
    loathing to-night hating him had let the child
    Christine
Play in the light of the lamp for hours after her bedtime;
    who fell asleep at length on the floor
Beside the dog; then Johnny: "Put her to bed." She
    gathered the child against her breasts, she laid her
In the next room, and covered her with a blanket. The
    window was white, the moon had risen. The mother
Lay down by the child, but after a moment Johnny stood
    in the doorway. "Come drink." He had brought
    home
Two jugs of wine slung from the saddle, part payment
    for the stallion's service; a pitcher of it
Was on the table, and California sadly came and emp-
    tied her glass. Whiskey, she thought,
Would have erased him till to-morrow; the thin red

wine. . . . "We have a good evening," he laughed,
  pouring it.
"One glass yet then I show you what the red fellow did."
  She moving toward the house-door his eyes
Followed her, the glass filled and the red juice ran over
  the table. When it struck the floor-planks
He heard and looked. "Who stuck the pig?" he muttered
  stupidly, "here's blood, here's blood," and trailed
  his fingers
In the red lake under the lamplight. While he was look-
  ing down the door creaked, she had slipped out-
  doors,
And he, his mouth curving like a faun's imagined the
  chase under the solemn redwoods, the panting
And unresistant victim caught in a dark corner. He emp-
  tied the glass and went outdoors
Into the dappled lanes of moonlight. No sound but the
  April brook's. "Hey Bruno," he called, "find her.
Bruno, go find her." The dog after a little understood
  and quested, the man following.
When California crouching by an oak-bush above the
  house heard them come near she darted
To the open slope and ran down hill. The dog barked
  at her heels, pleased with the game, and Johnny
Followed in silence. She ran down to the new corral, she
  saw the stallion
Move like a lion along the timbers of the fence, the dark
  arched neck shaking the nightfall
Of the great mane; she threw herself prone and writhed
  under the bars, his hooves backing away from her
Made muffled thunder in the soft soil. She stood in the
  midst of the corral, panting, but Johnny
Paused at the fence. The dog ran under it, and seeing
  the stallion move, the woman standing quiet,

Danced after the beast, with white-tooth feints and
    dashes. When Johnny saw the formidable dark
    strength
Recoil from the dog, he climbed up over the fence.
The child Christine waked when her mother left her
And lay half dreaming, in the half-waking dream she
    saw the ocean come up out of the west
And cover the world, she looked up through clear water
    at the tops of the redwoods. She heard the door
    creak
And the house empty; her heart shook her body, sitting
    up on the bed, and she heard the dog
And crept toward light, where it gleamed under the
    crack of the door. She opened the door, the room
    was empty,
The table-top was a red lake under the lamplight. The
    color of it was terrible to her;
She had seen the red juice drip from a coyote's muzzle
    her father had shot one day in the hills
And carried him home over the saddle: she looked at
    the rifle on the wall-rack: it was not moved:
She ran to the door, the dog was barking and the moon
    was shining: she knew wine by the odor
But the color frightened her, the empty house frightened
    her, she followed down hill in the white lane of
    moonlight
The friendly noise of the dog. She saw in the big horse's
    corral, on the level shoulder of the hill,
Black on white, the dark strength of the beast, the danc-
    ing fury of the dog, and the two others.
One fled, one followed; the big one charged, rearing; one
    fell under his fore-hooves. She heard her mother
Scream: without thought she ran to the house, she

dragged a chair past the red pool and climbed to the rifle,

Got it down from the wall and lugged it somehow through the door and down the hillside, under the hard weight

Sobbing. Her mother stood by the rails of the corral, she gave it to her. On the far side

The dog flashed at the plunging stallion; in the midst of the space the man, slow-moving, like a hurt worm

Crawling, dragged his body by inches toward the fence-line. Then California, resting the rifle

On the top rail, without doubting, without hesitance, Aimed for the leaping body of the dog, and when it stood, fired. It snapped, rolled over, lay quiet.

"O mother you've hit Bruno!" "I couldn't see the sights in the moonlight," she answered quietly. She stood

And watched, resting the rifle-butt on the ground. The stallion wheeled, freed from his torment, the man

Lurched up to his knees, wailing a thin and bitter bird's cry, and the roan thunder

Struck; hooves left nothing alive but teeth tore up the remnant. "O mother, shoot, shoot!" Yet California

Stood carefully watching, till the beast having fed all his fury stretched neck to utmost, head high,

And wrinkled back the upper lip from the teeth, yawning obscene disgust over—not a man—

A smear on the moon-like earth: then California moved by some obscure human fidelity

Lifted the rifle. Each separate nerve-cell of her brain flaming the stars fell from their places

Crying in her mind: she fired three times before the haunches crumpled sidewise, the forelegs stiffening,

And the beautiful strength settled to earth: she turned
    then on her little daughter the mask of a woman
Who has killed God. The night-wind veering, the smell
    of the spilt wine drifted down hill from the house.

✳ Woodrow Wilson

(*written February, 1924*)

It said "Come home, here is an end, a goal,
Not the one raced for, is it not better indeed? Victory
  you know requires
Force to sustain victory, the burden is never lightened,
  but final defeat
Buys peace: you have praised peace, peace without vic-
  tory."

He said "It seems I am traveling no new way,
But leaving my great work unfinished how can I rest? I
  enjoyed a vision,
Endured betrayal, you must not ask me to endure final
  defeat,
Visionless men, blind hearts, blind mouths, live still."

It said "Yet perhaps your vision was less great
Than some you scorned, it has not proved even so prac-
  ticable; Lenin
Enters this pass with less reluctance. As to betrayals:
  there are so many
Betrayals, the Russians and the Germans know."

He said "I knew I have enemies, I had not thought
To meet one at this brink: shall not the mocking voices
  die in the grave?"
It said "They shall. Soon there is silence." "I dreamed
  this end," he said, "when the prow
Of the long ship leaned against dawn, my people

Applauded me, and the world watched me. Again
I dreamed it at Versailles, the time I sent for the ship,
    and the obstinate foreheads
That shared with me the settlement of the world flinched
    at my threat and yielded.
That is all gone. . . . Do I remember this darkness?"

It said "No man forgets it but a moment.
The darkness before the mother, the depth of the re-
    turn." "I thought," he answered,
"That I was drawn out of this depth to establish the
    earth on peace. My labor
Dies with me, why was I drawn out of this depth?"

It said "Loyal to your highest, sensitive, brave,
Sanguine, some few ways wise, you and all men are
    drawn out of this depth
Only to be these things you are, as flowers for color,
    falcons for swiftness,
Mountains for mass and quiet. Each for its quality

Is drawn out of this depth. Your tragic quality
Required the huge delusion of some major purpose to
    produce it.
What, that the God of the stars needed your help?" He
    said "This is my last
Worst pain, the bitter enlightenment that buys peace."

✻ Boats in a Fog

Sports and gallantries, the stage, the arts, the antics of
  dancers,
The exuberant voices of music,
Have charm for children but lack nobility; it is bitter
  earnestness
That makes beauty; the mind
Knows, grown adult.
                  A sudden fog-drift muffled the
  ocean,
A throbbing of engines moved in it,
At length, a stone's throw out, between the rocks and
  the vapor,
One by one moved shadows
Out of the mystery, shadows, fishing-boats, trailing each
  other
Following the cliff for guidance,
Holding a difficult path between the peril of the sea-fog
And the foam on the shore granite.
One by one, trailing their leader, six crept by me,
Out of the vapor and into it,
The throb of their engines subdued by the fog, patient
  and cautious,
Coasting all round the peninsula
Back to the buoys in Monterey harbor. A flight of peli-
  cans
Is nothing lovelier to look at;
The flight of the planets is nothing nobler; all the arts
  lose virtue
Against the essential reality
Of creatures going about their business among the equally
Earnest elements of nature.

✳ Summer Holiday

When the sun shouts and people abound
One thinks there were the ages of stone and the age of
    bronze
And the iron age; iron the unstable metal;
Steel made of iron, unstable as his mother; the tow-
    ered-up cities
Will be stains of rust on mounds of plaster.
Roots will not pierce the heaps for a time, kind rains
    will cure them,
Then nothing will remain of the iron age
And all these people but a thigh-bone or so, a poem
Stuck in the world's thought, splinters of glass
In the rubbish dumps, a concrete dam far off in the
    mountain . . .

✳ Science

Man, introverted man, having crossed
In passage and but a little with the nature of things this
    latter century
Has begot giants; but being taken up
Like a maniac with self-love and inward conflicts can-
    not manage his hybrids.
Being used to deal with edgeless dreams,
Now he's bred knives on nature turns them also inward:
    they have thirsty points though.
His mind forebodes his own destruction;
Actæon who saw the goddess naked among leaves and
    his hounds tore him.
A little knowledge, a pebble from the shingle,
A drop from the oceans: who would have dreamed this
    infinitely little too much?

✳ The Torch-Bearers' Race

Here is the world's end. When our fathers forded the
    first river in Asia we crossed the world's end;
And when the North Sea throbbed under their keels, the
    world's end;
And when the Atlantic surge rolled English oak in the
    sea-trough; always there was farther to go,
A new world piecing out the old one: but ours, our new
    world?
Dark and enormous rolls the surf; down on the mystical
    tide-line under the cliffs at moonset
Dead tribes move, remembering the scent of their hills,
    the lost hunters
Our fathers hunted; they driven westward died the sun's
    death, they dread the depth and hang at the land's
    hem,
And are unavenged; frail ghosts, and ghostlike in their
    lives too,
Having only a simple hunger for all our complication of
    desires. Dark and enormous
Rolls the surf of the far storms of the heart of the ocean;
The old granite breaks into white torches the heavy-
    shouldered children of the wind . . . our ancient
    wanderings
West from the world's birth what sea-bound breaking
    shall flame up torchlike?
I am building a thick stone pillar upon this shore, the
    very turn of the world, the long migration's
End; the sun goes on but we have come up to an end.
We have climbed at length to a height, to an end, this
    end: shall we go down again to Mother Asia?
Some of us will go down, some will abide, but we sought

More than to return to a mother. This huge, inhuman,
    remote, unruled, this ocean will show us
The inhuman road, the unruled attempt, the remote lode-
    star.
The torch-bearers' race: it is run in a dusk; when the
    emptied racer drops unseen at the end of his course
A fresh hand snatches the hilt of the light, the torch flies
    onward
Though the man die. Not a runner knows where the light
    was lighted, not a runner knows where it carries
    fire to,
Hand kisses hand in the dark, the torch passes, the man
Falls, and the torch passes. It gleamed across Euphrates
    mud, shone on Nile shore, it lightened
The little homely Ionian water and the sweet Ægean.
O perfect breathing of the runners, those narrow courses,
    names like the stars' names, Sappho, Alcæus,
And Æschylus a name like the first eagle's; but the torch
    westering
The seas widened, the earth's bloom hardened, the stone
    rose Rome seeding the earth, but the torch norther-
    ing
Lightened the Atlantic . . . O flame, O beauty and
    shower of beauty,
There is yet one ocean and then no more, God whom
    you shine to walks there naked, on the final Pacific,
Not in a man's form.
            The torch answered: Have I kin-
    dled a morning?
For again, this old world's end is the gate of a world fire
    new, of your wild future, wild as a hawk's dream,
Ways hung on nothing, like stars, feet shaking earth off;
    that long way

Was a labor in a dream, will you wake now? The eaglets
    rustle in the aerie, the red eyes of dawn stabbing up
    through the nest-side,
You have walked in a dream, consumed with your fa-
    thers and your mothers, you have loved
Inside the four walls of humanity, passions turned in-
    ward, incestuous desires and a fighting against
    ghosts, but the clarions
Of light have called morning.
                        What, not to be tangled
    any more in the blinding
Rays of reflected desire, the man with the woman, the
    woman with the child, the daughter with the fa-
    ther, but freed
Of the web self-woven, the burning and the blistering
    strands running inward?
Those rays to be lightened awide, to shine up the star-
    path, subduing the world outward? Oh chicks in
    the high nest be fledged now,
Having found out flight in the air to make wing to the
    height, fierce eye-flames
Of the eaglets be strengthened, to drink of the fountain
    of the beauty of the sun of the stars, and to gaze
    in his face, not a father's,
And motherless and terrible and here.
                        But I at the gate,
    I falling
On the gate-sill add this: When the ancient wisdom is
    folded like a wine-stained cloth and laid up in dark-
    ness.
And the old symbols forgotten, in the glory of that your
    hawk's dream
Remember that the life of mankind is like the life of a
    man, a flutter from darkness to darkness

Across the bright hair of a fire, so much of the ancient
Knowledge will not be annulled. What unimaginable
    opponent to end you?
                        There is one fountain
Of power, yours and that last opponent's, and of long
    peace.

✳ Tor House

If you should look for this place after a handful of life-
  times:
Perhaps of my planted forest a few
May stand yet, dark-leaved Australians or the coast
  cypress, haggard
With storm-drift; but fire and the axe are devils.
Look for foundations of sea-worn granite, my fingers
  had the art
To make stone love stone, you will find some remnant.
But if you should look in your idleness after ten thou-
  sand years:
It is the granite knoll on the granite
And lava tongue in the midst of the bay, by the mouth of
  the Carmel
River-valley, these four will remain
In the change of names. You will know it by the wild sea-
  fragrance of wind
Though the ocean may have climbed or retired a little;
You will know it by the valley inland that our sun and
  our moon were born from
Before the poles changed; and Orion in December
Evenings was strung in the throat of the valley like a
  lamp-lighted bridge.
Come in the morning you will see white gulls
Weaving a dance over blue water, the wane of the moon
Their dance-companion, a ghost walking
By daylight, but wider and whiter than any bird in the
  world.
My ghost you needn't look for; it is probably
Here, but a dark one, deep in the granite, not dancing
  on wind
With the mad wings and the day moon.

✳ Hurt Hawks

I

The broken pillar of the wing jags from the clotted
    shoulder,
The wing trails like a banner in defeat,
No more to use the sky forever but live with famine
And pain a few days: cat nor coyote
Will shorten the week of waiting for death, there is game
    without talons.
He stands under the oak-bush and waits
The lame feet of salvation; at night he remembers free-
    dom
And flies in a dream, the dawns ruin it.
He is strong and pain is worse to the strong, incapacity
    is worse.
The curs of the day come and torment him
At distance, no one but death the redeemer will humble
    that head,
The intrepid readiness, the terrible eyes.
The wild God of the world is sometimes merciful to those
That ask mercy, not often to the arrogant.
You do not know him, you communal people, or you
    have forgotten him;
Intemperate and savage, the hawk remembers him;
Beautiful and wild, the hawks, and men that are dying,
    remember him.

II

I'd sooner, except the penalties, kill a man than a hawk;
    but the great redtail
Had nothing left but unable misery
From the bone too shattered for mending, the wing that
    trailed under his talons when he moved.

We had fed him six weeks, I gave him freedom,
He wandered over the foreland hill and returned in the
     evening, asking for death,
Not like a beggar, still eyed with the old
Implacable arrogance. I gave him the lead gift in the
     twilight. What fell was relaxed,
Owl-downy, soft feminine feathers; but what
Soared: the fierce rush: the night-herons by the flooded
     river cried fear at its rising
Before it was quite unsheathed from reality.

✳ Soliloquy

August and laurelled have been content to speak for an
    age, and the ages that follow
Respect them for that pious fidelity;
But you have disfeatured time for timelessness.
They had heroes for companions, beautiful youths to
    dream of, rose-marble-fingered
Women shed light down the great lines;
But you have invoked the slime in the skull,
The lymph in the vessels. They have shown men Gods
    like racial dreams, the woman's desire,
The man's fear, the hawk-faced prophet's; but nothing
Human seems happy at the feet of yours.
Therefore though not forgotten, not loved, in gray old
    years in the evening leaning
Over the gray stones of the tower-top,
You shall be called heartless and blind;
And watch new time answer old thought, not a face
    strange nor a pain astonishing;
But you living be laired in the rock
That sheds pleasure and pain like hailstones.

✳ An Artist

That sculptor we knew, the passionate-eyed son of a
    quarryman,
Who astonished Rome and Paris in his meteor youth,
    and then was gone, at his high tide of triumphs,
Without reason or good-bye; I have seen him again
    lately, after twenty years, but not in Europe.

In desert hills I rode a horse slack-kneed with thirst.
    Down a steep slope a dancing swarm
Of yellow butterflies over a shining rock made me hope
    water. We slid down to the place,
The spring was bitter but the horse drank. I imagined
    wearings of an old path from that wet rock
Ran down the canyon; I followed, soon they were lost,
    I came to a stone valley in which it seemed
No man nor his mount had ever ventured, you won-
    dered whether even a vulture'd ever spread sail
    there.
There were stones of strange form under a cleft in the
    far hill; I tethered the horse to a rock
And scrambled over. A heap like a stone torrent, a
    moraine,
But monstrously formed limbs of broken carving ap-
    peared in the rock-fall, enormous breasts, defaced
    heads
Of giants, the eyes calm through the brute veils of frac-
    ture. It was natural then to climb higher and go in
Up the cleft gate. The canyon was a sheer-walled crack
    winding at the entrance, but around its bend
The walls grew dreadful with stone giants, presences
    growing out of the rigid precipice, that strove
In dream between stone and life, intense to cast their

chaos . . . or to enter and return . . . stone-
fleshed, nerve-stretched
Great bodies ever more beautiful and more heavy with
pain, they seemed leading to some unbearable
Consummation of the ecstasy . . . but there, troll
among Titans, the bearded master of the place
accosted me
In a cold anger, a mallet in his hand, filthy and ragged.
There was no kindness in that man's mind,
But after he had driven me down to the entrance he
spoke a little.

> The merciless sun had found the slot
now
To hide in, and lit for the wick of that stone lamp-bowl
a sky almost, I thought, abominably beautiful;
While our lost artist we used to admire: for now I knew
him: spoke of his passion.

> He said, "Marble?
White marble is fit to model a snow-mountain: let man
be modest. Nor bronze: I am bound to have my
tool
In my material, no irrelevances. I found this pit of dark-
gray freestone, fine-grained, and tough enough
To make sketches that under any weathering will last my
lifetime. . . .

The town is eight miles off, I can fetch food and no one
follows me home. I have water and a cave
Here; and no possible lack of material. I need, therefore,
nothing. As to companions, I make them.
And models? They are seldom wanted; I know a Basque

shepherd I sometimes use; and a woman of the
town.
What more? Sympathy? Praise? I have never desired
them and also I have never deserved them. I will
not show you
More than the spalls you saw by accident.

What I see is
the enormous beauty of things, but what I attempt
Is nothing to that. I am helpless toward that.
It is only to form in stone the mould of some ideal hu-
manity that might be worthy to *be*
Under that lightning. Animalcules that God (if he were
given to laughter) might omit to laugh at.

Those children of my hands are tortured, because they
feel," he said, "the storm of the outer magnificence.
They are giants in agony. They have seen from my eyes
the man-destroying beauty of the dawns over their
notch yonder, and all the obliterating stars.
But in their eyes they have peace. I have lived a little and
I think
Peace marrying pain alone can breed that excellence in
the luckless race, might make it decent
To exist at all on the star-lit stone breast.

I hope," he
said, "that when I grow old and the chisel drops,
I may crawl out on a ledge of the rock and die like a
wolf."

These fragments are all I can remember,
These in the flare of the desert evening. Having been
driven so brutally forth I never returned;

Yet I respect him enough to keep his name and the place
   secret. I hope that some other traveller
May stumble on that ravine of Titans after their maker
   has died. While he lives, let him alone.

✳ Iona: The Graves of the Kings

I wish not to lie here.
There's hardly a plot of earth not blessed for burial, but
    here
One might dream badly.

In beautiful seas a beautiful
And sainted island, but the dark earth so shallow on the
    rock
Gorged with bad meat.

Kings buried in the lee of the saint,
Kings of fierce Norway, blood-boltered Scotland, bit-
    terly dreaming
Treacherous Ireland.

Imagine what delusions of grandeur,
What suspicion-agonized eyes, what jellies of arrogance
    and terror
This earth has absorbed.

✳ Shakespeare's Grave

"Doggerel," he thought, "will do for church-wardens,
Poetry's precious enough not to be wasted,"
And rhymed it all out with a skew smile:
"Spare these stones. Curst be he that moves my bones—
Will hold the hands of masons and grave-diggers."
But why did the good man care? For he wanted quiet-
    ness.
He had tasted enough life in his time
To stuff a thousand; he wanted not to swim wide
In waters, nor wander the enormous air,
Nor grow into grass, enter through the mouths of cattle
The bodies of lusty women and warriors,
But all he finished. He knew it feelingly; the game
Of the whirling circles had become tiresome.
"Annihilation's impossible, but insulated
In the church under the rhyming flagstone
Perhaps my passionate ruins may be kept off market
To the end of this age. Oh, a thousand years
Will hardly leach," he thought, "this dust of that fire."

* The Bed by the Window

I chose the bed downstairs by the sea-window for a good
    death-bed
When we built the house; it is ready waiting,
Unused unless by some guest in a twelvemonth, who
    hardly suspects
Its latter purpose. I often regard it,
With neither dislike nor desire; rather with both, so
    equalled
That they kill each other and a crystalline interest
Remains alone. We are safe to finish what we have to
    finish;
And then it will sound rather like music
When the patient daemon behind the screen of sea-rock
    and sky
Thumps with his staff, and calls thrice: "Come, Jeffers."

❋ The Place for No Story

The coast hills at Sovranes Creek:
No trees, but dark scant pasture drawn thin
Over rock shaped like flame;
The old ocean at the land's foot, the vast
Gray extension beyond the long white violence;
A herd of cows and the bull
Far distant, hardly apparent up the dark slope;
And the gray air haunted with hawks:
This place is the noblest thing I have ever seen.
                                        No imag-
      inable
Human presence here could do anything
But dilute the lonely self-watchful passion.

✳ Rock and Hawk

Here is a symbol in which
Many high tragic thoughts
Watch their own eyes.

This gray rock, standing tall
On the headland, where the seawind
Lets no tree grow,

Earthquake-proved, and signatured
By ages of storms: on its peak
A falcon has perched.

I think, here is your emblem
To hang in the future sky;
Not the cross, not the hive,

But this; bright power, dark peace;
Fierce consciousness joined with final
Disinterestedness;

Life with calm death; the falcon's
Realist eyes and act
Married to the massive

Mysticism of stone,
Which failure cannot cast down
Nor success make proud.

* Shine, Republic

The quality of these trees, green height; of the sky,
    shining, of water, a clear flow; of the rock, hardness
And reticence: each is noble in its quality. The love of
    freedom has been the quality of Western man.

There is a stubborn torch that flames from Marathon to
    Concord, its dangerous beauty binding three ages
Into one time; the waves of barbarism and civilization
    have eclipsed but have never quenched it.

For the Greeks the love of beauty, for Rome of ruling;
    for the present age the passionate love of discovery;
But in one noble passion we are one; and Washington,
    Luther, Tacitus, Aeschylus, one kind of man.

And you, America, that passion made you. You were
    not born to prosperity, you were born to love free-
    dom.
You did not say "en masse," you said "independence."
    But we cannot have all the luxuries and freedom
    also.

Freedom is poor and laborious; that torch is not safe but
    hungry, and often requires blood for its fuel.
You will tame it against it burn too clearly, you will hood
    it like a kept hawk, you will perch it on the wrist of
    Caesar.

But keep the tradition, conserve the forms, the ob-
    servances, keep the spot sore. Be great, carve deep
    your heel-marks.

The states of the next age will no doubt remember you,
and edge their love of freedom with contempt of
luxury.

✳ Love the Wild Swan

"I hate my verses, every line, every word.
Oh pale and brittle pencils ever to try
One grass-blade's curve, or the throat of one bird
That clings to twig, ruffled against white sky.
Oh cracked and twilight mirrors ever to catch
One color, one glinting flash, of the splendor of things.
Unlucky hunter, Oh bullets of wax,
The lion beauty, the wild-swan wings, the storm of the
       wings."
—This wild swan of a world is no hunter's game.
Better bullets than yours would miss the white breast,
Better mirrors than yours would crack in the flame.
Does it matter whether you hate your . . . self? At
       least
Love your eyes that can see, your mind that can
Hear the music, the thunder of the wings. Love the wild
       swan.

✳ Return

A little too abstract, a little too wise,
It is time for us to kiss the earth again,
It is time to let the leaves rain from the skies,
Let the rich life run to the roots again.
I will go down to the lovely Sur Rivers
And dip my arms in them up to the shoulders.
I will find my accounting where the alder leaf quivers
In the ocean wind over the river boulders.
I will touch things and things and no more thoughts,
That breed like mouthless May-flies darkening the sky,
The insect clouds that blind our passionate hawks
So that they cannot strike, hardly can fly.
Things are the hawk's food and noble is the mountain,
    Oh noble
Pico Blanco, steep sea-wave of marble.

✳ The Purse-Seine

Our sardine fishermen work at night in the dark of the
    moon; daylight or moonlight
They could not tell where to spread the net, unable to
    see the phosphorescence of the shoals of fish.
They work northward from Monterey, coasting Santa
    Cruz; off New Year's Point or off Pigeon Point
The look-out man will see some lakes of milk-color light
    on the sea's night-purple; he points, and the helms-
    man
Turns the dark prow, the motorboat circles the gleaming
    shoal and drifts out her seine-net. They close the
    circle
And purse the bottom of the net, then with great labor
    haul it in.

                I cannot tell you
How beautiful the scene is, and a little terrible, then,
    when the crowded fish
Know they are caught, and wildly beat from one wall to
    the other of their closing destiny the phosphorescent
Water to a pool of flame, each beautiful slender body
    sheeted with flame, like a live rocket
A comet's tail wake of clear yellow flame; while outside
    the narrowing
Floats and cordage of the net great sea-lions come up to
    watch, sighing in the dark; the vast walls of night
Stand erect to the stars.

                    Lately I was looking from a
night mountain-top
On a wide city, the colored splendor, galaxies of light:
    how could I help but recall the seine-net

Gathering the luminous fish? I cannot tell you how beau-
tiful the city appeared, and a little terrible.
I thought, We have geared the machines and locked all
together into interdependence; we have built the
great cities; now
There is no escape. We have gathered vast populations
incapable of free survival, insulated
From the strong earth, each person in himself helpless,
on all dependent. The circle is closed, and the net
Is being hauled in. They hardly feel the cords drawing,
yet they shine already. The inevitable mass-dis-
asters
Will not come in our time nor in our children's, but we
and our children
Must watch the net draw narrower, government take all
powers—or revolution, and the new government
Take more than all, add to kept bodies kept souls—or
anarchy, the mass-disasters.

                            These things are Prog-
ress;
Do you marvel our verse is troubled or frowning, while
it keeps its reason? Or it lets go, lets the mood flow
In the manner of the recent young men into mere hys-
teria, splintered gleams, crackled laughter. But they
are quite wrong.
There is no reason for amazement: surely one always
knew that cultures decay, and life's end is death.

✳ Prescription of Painful Ends

Lucretius felt the change of the world in his time, the
  great republic riding to the height
Whence every road leads downward; Plato in his time
  watched Athens
Dance the down path. The future is a misted landscape,
  no man sees clearly, but at cyclic turns
There is a change felt in the rhythm of events, as when
  an exhausted horse
Falters and recovers, then the rhythm of the running
  hoofbeats is changed: he will run miles yet,
But he must fall: we have felt it again in our own life
  time, slip, shift and speed-up
In the gallop of the world; and now perceive that, come
  peace or war, the progress of Europe and America
Becomes a long process of deterioration—starred with
  famous Byzantiums and Alexandrias,
Surely—but downward. One desires at such times
To gather the insights of the age summit against future
  loss, against the narrowing mind and the tyrants,
The pedants, the mystagogues, the barbarians: one
  builds poems for treasuries, time-conscious poems:
  Lucretius
Sings his great theory of natural origins and of wise
  conduct; Plato smiling carves dreams, bright cells
Of incorruptible wax to hive the Greek honey.
                              Our own
  time, much greater and far less fortunate,
Has acids for honey, and for fine dreams
The immense vulgarities of misapplied science and de-
  caying Christianity: therefore one christens each
  poem, in dutiful
Hope of burning off at least the top layer of the time's
  uncleanness, from the acid-bottles.

✳ Contemplation of the Sword

(*written April, 1938*)

Reason will not decide at last; the sword will decide.
The sword: an obsolete instrument of bronze or steel,
     formerly used to kill men, but here
In the sense of a symbol. The sword: that is: the storms
     and counter-storms of general destruction; killing
     of men,
Destruction of all goods and materials; massacre, more
     or less intentional, of children and women;
Destruction poured down from wings, the air made
     accomplice, the innocent air
Perverted into assassin and poisoner.

The sword: that is: treachery and cowardice, incredible
     baseness, incredible courage, loyalties, insanities.
The sword: weeping and despair, mass-enslavement,
     mass-torture, frustration of all the hopes
That starred man's forehead. Tyranny for freedom,
     horror for happiness, famine for bread, carrion for
     children.
Reason will not decide at last, the sword will decide.

Dear God, who are the whole splendor of things and the
     sacred stars, but also the cruelty and greed, the
     treacheries
And vileness, insanities and filth and anguish: now that
     this thing comes near us again I am finding it hard
To praise you with a whole heart.
                         I know what pain is,
     but pain can shine. I know what death is, I have
     sometimes

Longed for it. But cruelty and slavery and degradation,
    pestilence, filth, the pitifulness
Of men like little hurt birds and animals . . . if you
    were only
Waves beating rock, the wind and the iron-cored earth,
    the flaming insolent wildness of sun and stars,
With what a heart I could praise your beauty.
                            You will
    not repent, nor cancel life, nor free man from
    anguish
For many ages to come. You are the one that tortures
    himself to discover himself: I am
One that watches you and discovers you, and praises you
    in little parables, idyl or tragedy, beautiful
Intolerable God.
            The sword: that is:
I have two sons whom I love. They are twins, they were
    born in nineteen sixteen, which seemed to us a dark
    year
Of a great war, and they are now of the age
That war prefers. The first-born is like his mother, he is
    so beautiful
That persons I hardly know have stopped me on the
    street to speak of the grave beauty of the boy's face.
The second-born has strength for his beauty; when he
    strips for swimming the hero shoulders and wrestler
    loins
Make him seem clothed. The sword: that is: loathsome
    disfigurements, blindness, mutilation, locked lips of
    boys
Too proud to scream.
                Reason will not decide at last: the
    sword will decide.

✳ Be Angry at the Sun

That public men publish falsehoods
Is nothing new. That America must accept
Like the historical republics corruption and empire
Has been known for years.

Be angry at the sun for setting
If these things anger you. Watch the wheel slope and
    turn,
They are all bound on the wheel, these people, those
    warriors,
This republic, Europe, Asia.

Observe them gesticulating,
Observe them going down. The gang serves lies, the
    passionate
Man plays his part; the cold passion for truth
Hunts in no pack.

You are not Catullus, you know,
To lampoon these crude sketches of Caesar. You are far
From Dante's feet, but even farther from his dirty
Political hatreds.

Let boys want pleasure, and men
Struggle for power, and women perhaps for fame,
And the servile to serve a Leader and the dupes to be
    duped.
Yours is not theirs.

✳ For Una

I

I built her a tower when I was young—
Sometime she will die—
I built it with my hands, I hung
Stones in the sky.

Old but still strong I climb the stone—
Sometime she will die—
Climb the steep rough steps alone,
And weep in the sky.

Never weep, never weep.

2

Never be astonished, dear.
Expect change.
Nothing is strange.

We have seen the human race
Capture all its dreams,
All except peace.

We have watched mankind like Christ
Toil up and up,
To be hanged at the top.

No longer envying the birds,
That ancient prayer for
Wings granted: therefore

The heavy sky over London,
Stallion-hoofed,
Falls on the roofs.

These are the falling years,
They will go deep,
Never weep, never weep.

With clear eyes explore the pit.
Watch the great fall
With religious awe.

3

It is not Europe alone that is falling
Into blood and fire.
Decline and fall have been dancing in all men's souls
For a long while.

Sometime at the last gasp comes peace
To every soul.
Never to mine until I find out and speak
The things that I know.

4

Tomorrow I will take up that heavy poem again
About Ferguson, deceived and jealous man
Who bawled for the truth, the truth, and failed to endure
Its first least gleam. That poem bores me, and I hope will
    bore
Any sweet soul that reads it, being some ways
My very self but mostly my antipodes;
But having waved the heavy artillery to fire
I must hammer on to an end.

                    Tonight, dear,
Let's forget all that, that and the war,
And enisle ourselves a little beyond time,
You with this Irish whiskey, I with red wine,

While the stars go over the sleepless ocean,
And sometime after midnight I'll pluck you a wreath
Of chosen ones; we'll talk about love and death,
Rock-solid themes, old and deep as the sea,
Admit nothing more timely, nothing less real
While the stars go over the timeless ocean,
And when they vanish we'll have spent the night well.

* The House Dog's Grave

(Haig, an English bulldog)

I've changed my ways a little; I cannot now
Run with you in the evenings along the shore,
Except in a kind of dream; and you, if you dream a
 moment,
You see me there.

So leave awhile the paw-marks on the front door
Where I used to scratch to go out or in,
And you'd soon open; leave on the kitchen floor
The marks of my drinking-pan.

I cannot lie by your fire as I used to do
On the warm stone,
Nor at the foot of your bed; no, all the nights through
I lie alone.

But your kind thought has laid me less than six feet
Outside your window where firelight so often plays,
And where you sit to read—and I fear often grieving for
 me—
Every night your lamplight lies on my place.

You, man and woman, live so long, it is hard
To think of you ever dying.
A little dog would get tired, living so long.
I hope that when you are lying

Under the ground like me your lives will appear
As good and joyful as mine.

No, dears, that's too much hope: you are not so well
    cared for
As I have been.

And never have known the passionate undivided
Fidelities that I knew.
Your minds are perhaps too active, too many-sided. . . .
But to me you were true.

You were never masters, but friends. I was your friend.
I loved you well, and was loved. Deep love endures
To the end and far past the end. If this is my end,
I am not lonely. I am not afraid. I am still yours.

✻ The Excesses of God

Is it not by his high superfluousness we know
Our God? For to be equal a need
Is natural, animal, mineral: but to fling
Rainbows over the rain
And beauty above the moon, and secret rainbows
On the domes of deep sea-shells,
And make the necessary embrace of breeding
Beautiful also as fire,
Not even the weeds to multiply without blossom
Nor the birds without music:
There is the great humaneness at the heart of things,
The extravagant kindness, the fountain
Humanity can understand, and would flow likewise
If power and desire were perch-mates.

* The Sirens

Perhaps we desire death: or why is poison so sweet?
Why do the little Sirens
Make kindlier music, for a man caught in the net of the
   world
Between news-cast and work-desk—
The little chirping Sirens, alcohol, amusement, opiates,
And carefully sterilized lust—
Than the angels of life? Really it is rather strange, for
   the angels
Have all the power on their side,
All the importance:—men turn away from them, pre-
   ferring their own
Vulgar inventions, the little
Trivial Sirens. Here is another sign that the age needs
   renewal.

✳ Watch the Lights Fade

Gray steel, cloud-shadow-stained,
The ocean takes the last lights of evening.
Loud is the voice and the foam lead-color,
And flood-tide devours the sands.

Here stand, like an old stone,
And watch the lights fade and hear the sea's voice.
Hate and despair take Europe and Asia,
And the sea-wind blows cold.

Night comes: night will claim all.
The world is not changed, only more naked:
The strong struggle for power, and the weak
Warm their poor hearts with hate.

Night comes: come into the house,
Try around the dial for a late news-cast.
These others are America's voices: naive and
Powerful, spurious, doom-touched.

How soon? Four years or forty?
Why should an old stone pick at the future?
Stand on your shore, old stone, be still while the
Sea-wind salts your head white.

✳ The Soul's Desert

(*written August 30, 1939*)

They are warming up the old horrors; and all that they
    say is echoes of echoes.
Beware of taking sides; only watch.
These are not criminals, nor hucksters and little jour-
    nalists, but the governments
Of the great nations; men favorably
Representative of massed humanity. Observe them.
    Wrath and laughter
Are quite irrelevant. Clearly it is time
To become disillusioned, each person to enter his own
    soul's desert
And look for God—having seen man.

✳ The Bloody Sire

It is not bad. Let them play.
Let the guns bark and the bombing-plane
Speak his prodigious blasphemies.
It is not bad, it is high time,
Stark violence is still the sire of all the world's values.

What but the wolf's tooth whittled so fine
The fleet limbs of the antelope?
What but fear winged the birds, and hunger
Jeweled with such eyes the great goshawk's head?
Violence has been the sire of all the world's values.

Who would remember Helen's face
Lacking the terrible halo of spears?
Who formed Christ but Herod and Caesar,
The cruel and bloody victories of Caesar?
Violence, the bloody sire of all the world's values.

Never weep, let them play,
Old violence is not too old to beget new values.

✳ Their Beauty Has More Meaning

Yesterday morning enormous the moon hung low on the
    ocean,
Round and yellow-rose in the glow of dawn;
The night-herons flapping home wore dawn on their
    wings. Today
Black is the ocean, black and sulphur the sky,
And white seas leap. I honestly do not know which day
    is more beautiful.
I know that tomorrow or next year or in twenty years
I shall not see these things—and it does not matter, it
    does not hurt;
They will be here. And when the whole human race
Has been like me rubbed out, they will still be here:
    storms, moon and ocean,
Dawn and the birds. And I say this: their beauty has
    more meaning
Than the whole human race and the race of birds.

✳ Cassandra

The mad girl with the staring eyes and long white fingers
Hooked in the stones of the wall,
The storm-wrack hair and the screeching mouth: does it
    matter, Cassandra,
Whether the people believe
Your bitter fountain? Truly men hate the truth; they'd
    liefer
Meet a tiger on the road.
Therefore the poets honey their truth with lying; but
    religion-
Venders and political men
Pour from the barrel, new lies on the old, and are praised
    for kindly
Wisdom. Poor bitch, be wise.
No: you'll still mumble in a corner a crust of truth, to
    men
And gods disgusting.—You and I, Cassandra.

* Original Sin

The man-brained and man-handed ground-ape, phys-
 ically
The most repulsive of all hot-blooded animals
Up to that time of the world: they had dug a pitfall
And caught a mammoth, but how could their sticks and
 stones
Reach the life in that hide? They danced around the pit,
 shrieking
With ape excitement, flinging sharp flints in vain, and
 the stench of their bodies
Stained the white air of dawn; but presently one of them
Remembered the yellow dancer, wood-eating fire
That guards the cave-mouth: he ran and fetched him,
 and others
Gathered sticks at the wood's edge; they made a blaze
And pushed it into the pit, and they fed it high, around
 the mired sides
Of their huge prey. They watched the long hairy trunk
Waver over the stifle-trumpeting pain,
And they were happy.
                        Meanwhile the intense color and
  nobility of sunrise,
Rose and gold and amber, flowed up the sky. Wet rocks
  were shining, a little wind
Stirred the leaves of the forest and the marsh flag-flowers;
  the soft valley between the low hills
Became as beautiful as the sky; while in its midst, hour
  after hour, the happy hunters
Roasted their living meat slowly to death.
                                  These are the
  people.
This is the human dawn. As for me, I would rather

Be a worm in a wild apple than a son of man.
But we are what we are, and we might remember
Not to hate any person, for all are vicious;
And not be astonished at any evil, all are deserved;
And not fear death; it is the only way to be cleansed.

✳ The Inquisitors

Coming around a corner of the dark trail . . . what
    was wrong with the valley?
Azevedo checked his horse and sat staring: it was all
    changed. It was occupied. There were three hills
Where none had been: and firelight flickered red on
    their knees between them: if they were hills:
They were more like Red Indians around a camp-fire,
    grave and dark, mountain-high, hams on heels
Squatting around a little fire of hundred-foot logs. Aze-
    vedo remembers he felt an ice-brook
Glide on his spine; he slipped down from the saddle and
    hid
In the brush by the trail, above the black redwood forest.
    This was the Little Sur South Fork,
Its forest valley; the man had come in at nightfall over
    Bowcher's Gap, and a high moon hunted
Through running clouds. He heard the rumble of a
    voice, heavy not loud, saying, "I gathered some,
You can inspect them." One of the hills moved a huge
    hand
And poured its contents on a table-topped rock that
    stood in the firelight; men and women fell out;
Some crawled and some lay quiet; the hills leaned to eye
    them. One said: "It seems hardly possible
Such fragile creatures could be so noxious." Another
    answered,
"True, but we've seen. But it is only recently they have
    the power." The third answered, "That bomb?"
"Oh," he said, "—and the rest." He reached across and
    picked up one of the mites from the rock, and held it
Close to his eyes, and very carefully with finger and
    thumbnail peeled it: by chance a young female

With long black hair: it was too helpless even to scream.
He held it by one white leg and stared at it:
"I can see nothing strange: only so fragile." The third
hill answered, "We suppose it is something
Inside the head." Then the other split the skull with his
thumbnail, squinting his eyes and peering, and said,
"A drop of marrow. How could that spoil the earth?"
"Nevertheless," he answered,
"They have that bomb. The blasts and the fires are
nothing: freckles on the earth: the emanations
Might set the whole planet into a tricky fever
And destroy much." "Themselves," he answered. "Let
them. Why not?" "No," he answered, "life."

Azevedo
Still watched in horror, and all three of the hills
Picked little animals from the rock, peeled them and
cracked them, or toasted them
On the red coals, or split their bodies from the crotch up-
ward
To stare inside. They said, "It remains a mystery. How-
ever," they said,
"It is not likely they can destroy all life: the planet is
capacious. Life would surely grow up again
From grubs in the soil, or the newt and toad level, and
be beautiful again. And again perhaps break its legs
On its own cleverness: who can forecast the future?"
The speaker yawned, and with his flat hand
Brushed the rock clean; the three slowly stood up,
Taller than Pico Blanco into the sky, their Indian-beaked
heads in the moon-cloud,
And trampled their watchfire out and went away south-
ward, stepping across the Ventana mountains.

✳ Advice to Pilgrims

That our senses lie and our minds trick us is true, but in
    general
They are honest rustics; trust them a little;
The senses more than the mind, and your own mind more
    than another man's.
As to the mind's pilot, intuition—
Catch him clean and stark naked, he is first of truth-
    tellers; dream-clothed, or dirty
With fears and wishes, he is prince of liars.
The first fear is of death: trust no immortalist. The first
    desire
Is to be loved: trust no mother's son.
Finally I say let demagogues and world-redeemers bab-
    ble their emptiness
To empty ears; twice duped is too much.
Walk on gaunt shores and avoid the people; rock and
    wave are good prophets;
Wise are the wings of the gull, pleasant her song.

✳ Calm and Full the Ocean

Calm and full the ocean under the cool dark sky; quiet
    rocks and the birds fishing; the night-herons
Have flown home to their wood . . . while east and
    west in Europe and Asia and the islands unimagina-
    ble agonies

Consume mankind. Not a few thousand but uncounted
    millions, not a day but years, pain, horror, sick
    hatred;
Famine that dries the children to little bones and huge
    eyes; high explosive that fountains dirt, flesh and
    bone-splinters.

Sane and intact the seasons pursue their course, autumn
    slopes to December, the rains will fall
And the grass flourish, with flowers in it: as if man's
    world were perfectly separate from nature's, private
    and mad.

But that's not true; even the P-38s and the Flying
    Fortresses are as natural as horse-flies;
It is only that man, his griefs and rages, are not what
    they seem to man, not great and shattering, but
    really

Too small to produce any disturbance. This is good. This
    is the sanity, the mercy. It is true that the murdered
Cities leave marks in the earth for a certain time, like
    fossil rain-prints in shale, equally beautiful.

✳ The Eye

The Atlantic is a stormy moat; and the Mediterranean,
The blue pool in the old garden,
More than five thousand years has drunk sacrifice
Of ships and blood, and shines in the sun; but here the
    Pacific—
Our ships, planes, wars are perfectly irrelevant.
Neither our present blood-feud with the brave dwarfs
Nor any future world-quarrel of westering
And eastering man, the bloody migrations, greed of
    power, clash of faiths—
Is a speck of dust on the great scale-pan.
Here from this mountain shore, headland beyond stormy
    headland plunging like dolphins through the blue
    sea-smoke
Into pale sea—look west at the hill of water: it is half the
    planet: this dome, this half-globe, this bulging
Eyeball of water, arched over to Asia,
Australia and white Antarctica: those are the eyelids that
    never close; this is the staring unsleeping
Eye of the earth; and what it watches is not our wars.

✳ Teheran

The persons wane and fade, they fade out of meaning.
    Personal greatness
Was never more than a trick of the light, a halo of illu-
    sion—but who are these little smiling attendants
On a world's agony, meeting in Teheran to plot against
    whom what future? The future is clear enough,
In the firelight of burning cities and pain-light of that
    long battle-line,
That monstrous ulcer reaching from the Arctic Ocean to
    the Black Sea, slowly rodent westward: there will
    be Russia
And America; two powers alone in the world; two bulls
    in one pasture. And what is unlucky Germany
Between those foreheads?
                        Observe also
How rapidly civilization coarsens and decays; its better
    qualities, foresight, humaneness, disinterested
Respect for truth, die first; its worst will be last.—Oh,
    well: the future! When man stinks, turn to God.

✷ So Many Blood-Lakes

(*written May 12, 1944*)

We have now won two world-wars, neither of which
    concerned us, we were slipped in. We have levelled
    the powers
Of Europe, that were the powers of the world, into rub-
    ble and dependence. We have won two wars and a
    third is coming.

This one—will not be so easy. We were at ease while the
    powers of the world were split into factions: we've
    changed that.
We have enjoyed fine dreams; we have dreamed of unify-
    ing the world; we are unifying it—against us.

Two wars, and they breed a third. Now guard the beaches,
    watch the north, trust not the dawns. Probe every
    cloud.
Build power. Fortress America may yet for a long time
    stand, between the east and the west, like By-
    zantium.

—As for me: laugh at me. I agree with you. It is a fool-
    ish business to see the future and screech at it.
One should watch and not speak. And patriotism has run
    the world through so many blood-lakes: and we
    always fall in.

✳ Diagram

Look, there are two curves in the air: the air
That man's fate breathes: there is the rise and fall of
the Christian culture-complex, that broke its dawn-
cloud
Fifteen centuries ago, and now past noon
Drifts to decline; and there's the yet vaster curve, but
mostly in the future, of the age that began at Kitty-
hawk
Within one's lifetime.—The first of these curves passing
its noon and the second orient
All in one's little lifetime make it seem pivotal.
Truly the time is marked by insane splendors and ag-
onies. But watch when the two curves cross: you
children
Not far away down the hawk's-nightmare future: you
will see monsters.

✳ We Are Those People

I have abhorred the wars and despised the liars, laughed
    at the frightened
And forecast victory; never one moment's doubt.
But now not far, over the backs of some crawling years,
    the next
Great war's column of dust and fire writhes
Up the sides of the sky: it becomes clear that we too
    may suffer
What others have, the brutal horror of defeat—
Or if not in the next, then in the next—therefore watch
    Germany
And read the future. We wish, of course, that our women
Would die like biting rats in the cellars, our men like
    wolves on the mountain:
It will not be so. Our men will curse, cringe, obey;
Our women uncover themselves to the grinning victors
    for bits of chocolate.

* The World's Wonders

Being now three or four years more than sixty,
I have seen strange things in my time. I have seen a
    merman standing waist-deep in the ocean off my
    rock shore,

Unmistakably human and unmistakably a sea-beast: he
    submerged and never came up again,
While we stood watching. I do not know what he was,
    and I have no theory: but this was the least of
    wonders.

I have seen the United States grow up the strongest and
    wealthiest of nations, and swim in the wind over
    bankruptcy.
I have seen Europe, for twenty-five hundred years the
    crown of the world, become its beggar and cripple.

I have seen my people, fooled by ambitious men and a
    froth of sentiment, waste themselves on three wars.
None was required, all futile, all grandly victorious. A
    fourth is forming.

I have seen the invention of human flight; a chief desire
    of man's dreaming heart for ten thousand years;
And men have made it the chief of the means of mas-
    sacre.

I have seen the far stars weighed and their distance
    measured, and the powers that make the atom put
    into service—
For what?—To kill. To kill half a million flies—men I
    should say—at one slap.

I have also seen doom. You can stand up and struggle
   or lie down and sleep—you are doomed as Oedipus.
A man and a civilization grow old, grow fatally—as we
   say—ill: courage and the will are bystanders.

It is easy to know the beauty of inhuman things, sea,
   storm and mountain; it is their soul and their
   meaning.
Humanity has its lesser beauty, impure and painful; we
   have to harden our hearts to bear it.

I have hardened my heart only a little: I have learned
   that happiness is important, but pain *gives* im-
   portance.
The use of tragedy: Lear becomes as tall as the storm he
   crawls in; and a tortured Jew became God.

✳ The Old Stonemason

Stones that rolled in the sea for a thousand years
Have climbed the cliff and stand stiff-ranked in the
    house-walls;
Hurricane may spit his lungs out they'll not be moved.
They have become conservative; they remember the end-
    less
Treacheries of ever-sliding water and slimy ambushes
Along the shore; they'll never again give themselves
To the tides and the dreams, the popular drift,
The whirlpool progress, but stand steady on their hill—
At bay?—Yes; but unbroken.
                        I have much in common
        with these old rockheads.
Old comrades, I too have escaped and stand.
I have shared in my time the human illusions, the muddy
    foolishness
And craving passions, but something thirty years ago
    pulled me
Out of the tide-wash; I must not even pretend
To be one of the people. I must stand here
Alone with open eyes in the clear air growing old,
Watching with interest and only a little nausea
The cheating shepherds, this time of the demagogues
    and the docile people, the shifts of power,
And pitiless general wars that prepare the fall;
But also the enormous unhuman beauty of things; rock,
    sea and stars, fool-proof and permanent,
The birds like yachts in the air, or beating like hearts
Along the water; the flares of sunset, the peaks of Point
    Lobos;
And hear at night the huge waves, my drunken quarry-
    men

Climbing the cliff, hewing out more stones for me
To make my house. The old granite stones, those are
    my people;
Hard heads and stiff wits but faithful, not fools, not
    chatterers;
And the place where they stand today they will stand
    also tomorrow.

✳ The Beauty of Things

To feel and speak the astonishing beauty of things—
     earth, stone and water,
Beast, man and woman, sun, moon and stars—
The blood-shot beauty of human nature, its thoughts,
     frenzies and passions,
And unhuman nature its towering reality—
For man's half dream; man, you might say, is nature
     dreaming, but rock
And water and sky are constant—to feel
Greatly, and understand greatly, and express greatly, the
     natural
Beauty, is the sole business of poetry.
The rest's diversion: those holy or noble sentiments, the
     intricate ideas,
The love, lust, longing: reasons, but not the reason.

❋ Animals

At dawn a knot of sea-lions lies off the shore
In the slow swell between the rock and the cliff,
Sharp flippers lifted, or great-eyed heads, as they roll
    in the sea,
Bigger than draft-horses, and barking like dogs
Their all-night song. It makes me wonder a little
That life near kin to human, intelligent, hot-blooded,
    idle and singing, can float at ease
In the ice-cold midwinter water. Then, yellow dawn
Colors the south, I think about the rapid and furious
    lives in the sun:
They have little to do with ours; they have nothing to
    do with oxygen and salted water; they would look
    monstrous
If we could see them: the beautiful passionate bodies
    of living flame, batlike flapping and screaming,
Tortured with burning lust and acute awareness, that
    ride the storm-tides
Of the great fire-globe. They are animals, as we are.
    There are many other chemistries of animal life
Besides the slow oxidation of carbohydrates and amino-
    acids.

✳ To Death

I think of you as a great king, cold and austere;
The throne is not gold but iron, the stones of the high
    hall are black basalt blocks, and the pavement also,
With blood in the corners:
Yet you are merciful; it is for you we labor,
And after a time you give us eternal peace.

I think of you as a mean little servant, but steward of
    the estate,
Pale and a hunchback, shuffling along the corridors,
Tapping at every door. You have the keys of the
    treasury.

You are the arbiter of the games and bestower of prizes.
For you the young men sweat and the boys play battle,
    for your award
Their hot young lives: what can they win with their
    lives—
Whether they bide at home or bleed on the capes of
    Asia,
Or add columns of figures or the fates of Europe—
But eternal peace?
You sit and watch men fighting, and to you they come.
You watch the victors go home, and to you they come.

You have a sister named Life, an opulent treacherous
    woman,
Blonde and a harlot, a great promiser, and very cruel
    too.
Even the meanest minds after some time
Understand her tricks and her guile. You have a cousin
    named Christ

To whom men turn; but presently all to you. To you
    the conquerors
And to you the pale saints. The lions of the desert
And the sky-swimming eagles flock to your feet. Athens
    and Rome
Turned to adore you; and America will, no doubt of
    that:
We are intelligent too; we shall turn and bow down our
    heads.

✳ Morro Bay

Beautiful years when she was by me and we visited
Every rock and creek of the coast—
She gave life from her eyes. Now the bay is brown-
stagnant
With rotting weed, and the stranded fish-boats
Reek in the sun; but still the great rock hangs like a
thundercloud
Over the stale mist and still sea.
They say that it swarms with rattlesnakes—right—the
stored lightnings
In the stone cloud. Guard it well, vipers.
That Norman rockhead Mont St. Michel may have been
as beautiful as this one
Once, long ago, before it was built on.

✳ Skunks

The corruptions of war and peace, the public and whole-
    sale crimes that make war, the greed and lies of the
    peace
And victor's vengeance: how at a distance
They soften into romance—blue mountains and blos-
    somed marshes in the long landscape of history—
    Caligula
Becomes an amusing clown, and Genghiz
A mere genius, a great author of tragedies. Our own
    time's chiefs of massacre—Stalin died yesterday—
Watch how soon blood will bleach, and gross horror
Become words in a book.
                      We have little animals here,
    slow-stepping cousins of stoat and weasel,
Striped skunks, that can spit from under their tails
An odor so vile and stifling that neither wolf nor wild-
    cat dares to come near them; they walk in confi-
    dence,
Solely armed with this loathsome poison-gas.
But smelled far off—have you noticed?—it is surpris-
    ingly pleasant.
                  It is like the breath of ferns and wet
    earth
Deep in a wooded glen in the evening,
Cool water glides quietly over the moss-grown stones,
    quick trout dimple the pool.—Distance makes clean.

✳ The Deer Lay Down Their Bones

I followed the narrow cliffside trail half way up the
    mountain
Above the deep river-canyon. There was a little cataract
    crossed the path, flinging itself
Over tree roots and rocks, shaking the jeweled fern-
    fronds, bright bubbling water
Pure from the mountain, but a bad smell came up.
    Wondering at it I clambered down the steep stream
Some forty feet, and found in the midst of bush-oak and
    laurel,
Hung like a bird's nest on the precipice brink a small
    hidden clearing,
Grass and a shallow pool. But all about there were bones
    lying in the grass, clean bones and stinking bones,
Antlers and bones: I understood that the place was a
    refuge for wounded deer; there are so many
Hurt ones escape the hunters and limp away to lie hid-
    den; here they have water for the awful thirst
And peace to die in; dense green laurel and grim cliff
Make sanctuary, and a sweet wind blows upward from
    the deep gorge.—I wish my bones were with theirs.
But that's a foolish thing to confess, and a little cow-
    ardly. We know that life
Is on the whole quite equally good and bad, mostly gray
    neutral, and can be endured
To the dim end, no matter what magic of grass, water
    and precipice, and pain of wounds,
Makes death look dear. We have been given life and
    have used it—not a great gift perhaps—but in
    honesty
Should use it all. Mine's empty since my love died—

Empty? The flame-haired grandchild with great
blue eyes
That look like hers? —What can I do for the child? I
gaze at her and wonder what sort of man
In the fall of the world . . . I am growing old, that is
the trouble. My children and little grandchildren
Will find their way, and why should I wait ten years yet,
having lived sixty-seven, ten years more or less,
Before I crawl out on a ledge of rock and die snapping,
like a wolf
Who has lost his mate? —I am bound by my own thirty-
year-old decision: who drinks the wine
Should take the dregs; even in the bitter lees and sedi-
ment
New discovery may lie. The deer in that beautiful place
lay down their bones: I must wear mine.

✳ Carmel Point

The extraordinary patience of things!
This beautiful place defaced with a crop of surburban
    houses—
How beautiful when we first beheld it,
Unbroken field of poppy and lupin walled with clean
    cliffs;
No intrusion but two or three horses pasturing,
Or a few milch cows rubbing their flanks on the outcrop
    rockheads—
Now the spoiler has come: does it care?
Not faintly. It has all time. It knows the people are a tide
That swells and in time will ebb, and all
Their works dissolve. Meanwhile the image of the pris-
    tine beauty
Lives in the very grain of the granite,
Safe as the endless ocean that climbs our cliff. —As for
    us:
We must uncenter our minds from ourselves;
We must unhumanize our views a little, and become
    confident
As the rock and ocean that we were made from.

✳ De Rerum Virtute

I

Here is the skull of a man: a man's thoughts and emo-
    tions
Have moved under the thin bone vault like clouds
Under the blue one: love and desire and pain,
Thunderclouds of wrath and white gales of fear
Have hung inside here: and sometimes the curious de-
    sire of knowing
Values and purpose and the causes of things
Has coasted like a little observer airplane over the im-
    ages
That filled this mind: it never discovered much,
And now all's empty, a bone bubble, a blown-out egg-
    shell.

II

That's what it's like: for the egg too has a mind,
Doing what our able chemists will never do,
Building the body of a hatchling, choosing among the
    proteins:
These for the young wing-muscles, these for the great
Crystalline eyes, these for the flighty nerves and brain:
Choosing and forming: a limited but superhuman intelli-
    gence,
Prophetic of the future and aware of the past:
The hawk's egg will make a hawk, and the serpent's
A gliding serpent: but each with a little difference
From its ancestors—and slowly, if it works, the race
Forms a new race: that also is a part of the plan
Within the egg. I believe the first living cell
Had echoes of the future in it, and felt
Direction and the great animals, the deep green forest

And whale's-track sea; I believe this globed earth
Not all by chance and fortune brings forth her broods,
But feels and chooses. And the Galaxy, the firewheel
On which we are pinned, the whirlwind of stars in which
     our sun is one dust-grain, one electron, this giant
     atom of the universe
Is not blind force, but fulfils its life and intends its
     courses. "All things are full of God.
Winter and summer, day and night, war and peace are
     God."

III

Thus the thing stands; the labor and the games go on—
What for? What for? —Am I a god that I should know?
Men live in peace and happiness; men live in horror
And die howling. Do you think the blithe sun
Is ignorant that black waste and beggarly blindness trail
     him like hounds,
And will have him at last? He will be strangled
Among his dead satellites, remembering magnificence.

IV

I stand on the cliff at Sovranes creek-mouth.
Westward beyond the raging water and the bent shoulder
     of the world
The bitter futile war in Korea proceeds, like an idiot
Prophesying. It is too hot in mind
For anyone, except God perhaps, to see beauty in it. In-
     deed it is hard to see beauty
In any of the acts of man: but that means the acts of a
     sick microbe
On a satellite of a dust-grain twirled in a whirlwind
In the world of stars. . . .
Something perhaps may come of him; in any event

He can't last long. —Well: I am short of patience
Since my wife died . . . and this era of spite and hate-
    filled half-worlds
Gets to the bone. I believe that man too is beautiful,
But it is hard to see, and wrapped up in falsehoods.
   Michelangelo and the Greek sculptors—
How they flattered the race! Homer and Shakespeare—
How they flattered the race!

V

One light is left us: the beauty of things, not men;
The immense beauty of the world, not the human world.
Look—and without imagination, desire nor dream—
    directly
At the mountains and sea. Are they not beautiful?
These plunging promontories and flame-shaped peaks
Stopping the somber stupendous glory, the storm-fed
    ocean?
             Look at the Lobos Rocks off the shore,
With foam flying at their flanks, and the long sea-lions
Couching on them. Look at the gulls on the cliff-wind,
And the soaring hawk under the cloud-stream—
But in the sagebrush desert, all one sun-stricken
Color of dust, or in the reeking tropical rain-forest,
Or in the intolerant north and high thrones of ice—is
    the earth not beautiful?
Nor the great skies over the earth?
The beauty of things means virtue and value in them.
It is in the beholder's eye, not the world? Certainly.
It is the human mind's translation of the transhuman
Intrinsic glory. It means that the world is sound,
Whatever the sick microbe does. But he too is part of it.

✳ Let Them Alone

If God has been good enough to give you a poet
Then listen to him. But for God's sake let him alone un-
    til he is dead; no prizes, no ceremony,
They kill the man. A poet is one who listens
To nature and his own heart; and if the noise of the
    world grows up around him, and if he is tough
    enough,
He can shake off his enemies but not his friends.
That is what withered Wordsworth and muffled Tenny-
    son, and would have killed Keats; that is what
    makes
Hemingway play the fool and Faulkner forget his art.

✳ Vulture

I had walked since dawn and lay down to rest on a bare
hillside
Above the ocean. I saw through half-shut eyelids a vul-
ture wheeling high up in heaven,
And presently it passed again, but lower and nearer, its
orbit narrowing, I understood then
That I was under inspection. I lay death-still and heard
the flight-feathers
Whistle above me and make their circle and come
nearer.
I could see the naked red head between the great wings
Bear downward staring. I said, "My dear bird, we are
wasting time here.
These old bones will still work; they are not for you."
But how beautiful he looked, gliding down
On those great sails; how beautiful he looked, veering
away in the sea-light over the precipice. I tell you
solemnly
That I was sorry to have disappointed him. To be eaten
by that beak and become part of him, to share those
wings and those eyes—
What a sublime end of one's body, what an enskyment;
What a life after death.

✳ Birds and Fishes

Every October millions of little fish come along the
    shore,
Coasting this granite edge of the continent
On their lawful occasions: but what a festival for the sea-
    fowl.
What a witches' sabbath of wings
Hides the dark water. The heavy pelicans shout "Haw!"
    like Job's friend's warhorse
And dive from the high air, the cormorants
Slip their long black bodies under the water and hunt
    like wolves
Through the green half-light. Screaming, the gulls watch,
Wild with envy and malice, cursing and snatching. What
    hysterical greed!
What a filling of pouches! the mob
Hysteria is nearly human—these decent birds!—as if
    they were finding
Gold in the street. It is better than gold,
It can be eaten: and which one in all this fury of wild-
    fowl pities the fish?
No one certainly. Justice and mercy
Are human dreams, they do not concern the birds nor
    the fish nor eternal God.
However—look again before you go.
The wings and the wild hungers, the wave-worn skerries,
    the bright quick minnows
Living in terror to die in torment—
Man's fate and theirs—and the island rocks and im-
    mense ocean beyond, and Lobos
Darkening above the bay: they are beautiful?
That is their quality: not mercy, not mind, not goodness,
    but the beauty of God.

✳ Index of First Lines

✳ Index of Titles

ROBINSON JEFFERS died in 1962 at the age of seventy-five, ending one of the most controversial poetic careers of this century.

The son of a theology professor at Western Seminary in Pittsburgh, Jeffers was taught Greek, Latin, and Hebrew as a boy, and spent three years in Germany and Switzerland before entering the University of Pennsylvania (now Pittsburgh) at fifteen. His education continued on the West Coast after his parents moved there, and he received a B.A. from Occidental College at eighteen. His interest in forestry, medicine, and general science led him to pursue his studies at the University of Southern California and the University of Zurich.

The poems in this volume have been selected from his major works, among them *Be Angry at the Sun, Hungerfield, The Double Axe, The Beginning and the End,* and *Roan Stallion, Tamar and Other Poems.* His adaptation of *Medea* was successfully presented on Broadway.

VINTAGE FICTION, POETRY, AND PLAYS

V-814   **ABE, KOBO** / The Woman in the Dunes
V-2014   **AUDEN, W. H.** / Collected Longer Poems
V-2015   **AUDEN, W. H.** / Collected Shorter Poems 1927-1957
V-102   **AUDEN, W. H.** / Selected Poetry of W. H. Auden
V-601   **AUDEN, W. H. AND PAUL B. TAYLOR (trans.)** / The Elder Edda
V-20   **BABIN, MARIA-THERESA AND STAN STEINER (eds.)** / Borinquen: An Anthology of Puerto-Rican Literature
V-271   **BEDIER, JOSEPH** / Tristan and Iseult
V-523   **BELLAMY, JOE DAVID (ed.)** / Superfiction or The American Story Transformed: An Anthology
V-72   **BERNIKOW, LOUISE (ed.)** / The World Split Open: Four Centuries of Women Poets in England and America 1552-1950
V-321   **BOLT, ROBERT** / A Man for All Seasons
V-21   **BOWEN, ELIZABETH** / The Death of the Heart
V-294   **BRADBURY, RAY** / The Vintage Bradbury
V-670   **BRECHT, BERTOLT (ed. by Ralph Manheim and John Willett)** / Collected Plays, Vol. 1
V-759   **BRECHT, BERTOLT (ed. by Ralph Manheim and John Willett)** / Collected Plays, Vol. 5
V-216   **BRECHT, BERTOLT (ed. by Ralph Manheim and John Willett)** / Collected Plays, Vol. 7
V-819   **BRECHT, BERTOLT (ed. by Ralph Manheim and John Willett)** / Collected Plays, Vol. 9
V-841   **BYNNER, WITTER AND KIANG KANG-HU (eds.)** / The Jade Mountain: A Chinese Anthology
V-207   **CAMUS, ALBERT** / Caligula & Three Other Plays
V-281   **CAMUS, ALBERT** / Exile and the Kingdom
V-223   **CAMUS, ALBERT** / The Fall
V-865   **CAMUS, ALBERT** / A Happy Death: A Novel
V-626   **CAMUS, ALBERT** / Lyrical and Critical Essays
V-75   **CAMUS, ALBERT** / The Myth of Sisyphus and Other Essays
V-258   **CAMUS, ALBERT** / The Plague
V-245   **CAMUS, ALBERT** / The Possessed
V-30   **CAMUS, ALBERT** / The Rebel
V-2   **CAMUS, ALBERT** / The Stranger
V-28   **CATHER, WILLA** / Five Stories
V-705   **CATHER, WILLA** / A Lost Lady
V-200   **CATHER, WILLA** / My Mortal Enemy
V-179   **CATHER, WILLA** / Obscure Destinies
V-252   **CATHER, WILLA** / One of Ours
V-913   **CATHER, WILLA** / The Professor's House
V-434   **CATHER, WILLA** / Sapphira and the Slave Girl
V-680   **CATHER, WILLA** / Shadows on the Rock
V-684   **CATHER, WILLA** / Youth and the Bright Medusa
V-140   **CERF, BENNETT (ed.)** / Famous Ghost Stories
V-203   **CERF, BENNETT (ed.)** / Four Contemporary American Plays
V-127   **CERF, BENNETT (ed.)** / Great Modern Short Stories
V-326   **CERF, CHRISTOPHER (ed.)** / The Vintage Anthology of Science Fantasy